D1642655

[w

ABBEY THEATRE
TALES OF BALLYCUMBER
SEBASTIAN BARRY

Tales of Ballycumber by Sebastian Barry was premiered at
the Abbey Theatre on 7 October 2009.

The Abbey Theatre gratefully acknowledges the financial
support of the Arts Council / An Chomhairle Ealaíon.

This production runs without an interval

CAST (*in order of appearance*)

Girl	Lisa Hogg
Nicholas	Stephen Rea
Evans	Aaron Monaghan
Andrew	Dessie Gallagher
Tania	Derbhle Crotty

Director	David Leveaux
Set and Costume Design	Mike Britton
Lighting Design	Matthew Richardson
Composer	Corin Buckeridge
Sound Design	Ben Delaney
Video Design	Dick Straker for Mesmer
Dialect Coach	Brendan Gunn
Assistant Director	Sophie Motley
Company Stage Manager	Brendan Galvin
Deputy Stage Manager	Tara Furlong
Assistant Stage Manager	Elaine Walsh
Voice Director	Andrea Ainsworth
Casting Director	Holly Ní Chiardha (CDG)
Hair and Make-up	Val Sherlock
Photography	Ros Kavanagh
Graphic Design	Zero-G
Sign Language Interpreter	Amanda Coogan
Captioning	Ruth McCreery
	Paula McRedmond

Tales of Ballycumber by Sebastian Barry is an Abbey Theatre commission.

Please note that the text of the play which appears in this volume may be changed during the rehearsal process and appear in a slightly altered form in performance.

Audio described and captioned performances are provided by Arts and Disability Ireland with funding from the Arts Council / An Chomhairle Ealaíon.

Special thanks to Dana Lazyk from Flowers by Design.

ABBEY THEATRE
TALES OF BALLYCUMBER
SEBASTIAN BARRY

SEBASTIAN BARRY
WRITER

Sebastian Barry was born in 1955 in Dublin and educated at the Catholic University School and Trinity College Dublin. He recently received a Lord Mayor's Award for his services to Dublin and Literature. His plays include *Boss Grady's Boys* (1988), *Prayers of Sherkin* (1990), *White Woman Street* (1992), *The Only True History of Lizzie Finn* (1995), *The Steward of Christendom* (1995), *Our Lady of Sligo* (1998), *Hinterland* (2002), *Fred and Jane* (2002), *Whistling Psyche* (2004), *The Pride of Parnell Street* (2007) and *Dallas Sweetman* (2008). His novels include *The Whereabouts of Eneas McNulty* (1998), *Annie Dunne* (2002), *A Long Long Way* (2005) and *The Secret Scripture* (2008). His many awards include the Irish-America Fund Literary Award, the Christopher Ewart-Biggs Memorial Prize, the London Critics' Circle Award and the Kerry Group Irish Fiction Award. *A Long Long Way*, which was shortlisted for the Man Booker and the Dublin International Impac Prize, was the *Dublin: One City One Book* choice for 2007. *The Secret Scripture* was shortlisted for the Man Booker Prize and won the 2008 Costa Novel Award. He lives in Wicklow with his wife Alison and three children.

Welcome
Fáilte

The Abbey Theatre opened its doors on Abbey Street on 27 December 1904, with W. B. Yeats and Lady Augusta Gregory as its directors. Its precursors were the Irish Literary Theatre and Frank and Willie Fay's National Dramatic Society. The company originally traded as the National Theatre Society Limited. On 31st January 2006 this company was dissolved and a new company established, Abbey Theatre Amharclann Na Mainistreach, which now runs the theatre. The artistic policy of the Abbey remains unchanged and incorporates the following ambitions:

- *Invest in and promote new Irish writers and artists*
- *Produce an annual programme of diverse, engaging, innovative Irish and international theatre*
- *Attract and engage a broad range of customers and provide compelling experiences that inspire them to return*
- *Create a dynamic working environment which delivers world best practice across our business*

In 1925, the Abbey Theatre was given an annual subsidy by the new Free State, becoming the first ever state-subsidised theatre in the English speaking world. The Arts Council of Ireland/An Chomhairle Ealaíon, along with our friends, patrons, benefactors and you, our audience, continues to support our work.

In 1951, the original buildings of the Abbey Theatre were damaged by fire. The Abbey re-located to the Queen's Theatre. Fifteen years to the day later, on 18 July 1966, the Abbey moved back to its current home, designed by Michael Scott, on the same site.

In September 2006 the Government announced that an international design competition would be held to create a new home for the Abbey, to be located at George's Dock in Dublin. In October 2007 the jury for the competition was announced.

In the meantime, we have undertaken a programme of refurbishment and upgrade to enhance the experience for our artists and for you, the audience. This included the radical and widely welcomed reconfiguration of the Abbey auditorium.

Thank you for joining us for this production. We hope you enjoy the show and look forward to welcoming you again soon to the Abbey.

Osclaíodh doirse **Amharclann na Mainistreach** ar Shráid na Mainistreach ar an 27 Mí na Nollag 1904, le W. B. Yeats agus Bean Augusta Gregory mar stiúrthóirí. Ba iad a réamhtheachtaithe ná Amharclann Liteartha na hÉireann agus Cumann Drámata Náisiúnta Frank agus Willie Fay. Ar an 31 Mí Eanáir 2006 rinneadh an chuideachta seo a dhíscaoileadh agus bunaíodh cuideachta nua, Abbey Theatre Amharclann Na Mainistreach, a reáchtálann an amharclann anois. Níor tháinig aon athrú ar bheartas ealaíne Amharclann na Mainistreach go fóill agus cuimsíonn sé na spriocanna seo a leanas:

- *Chun infheistíocht a dhéanamh i scríbhneoirí agus in ealaíontóirí nua Éireannacha mar aon le hiad a chur chun cinn*
- *Chun clár bliantúil de drámaíocht Éireannach agus idirnásiúnta a sholáthar atá éagsúil, tarraingteach agus nuálach.*
- *Chun réimse leathan custaiméirí a mhealladh is a ghníomhú agus chun eispéiris spreagúla, a thugann orthu teacht ar ais, a sholáthar*
- *Chun timpeallacht oibre bhríomhar a chruthú a sholáthraíonn cleachtas scothdomhanda ar fud ár ngnó*

I 1925, thug Saorstát nua na hÉireann fóirdheontas bliantúil neamhghnách d'Amharclann na Mainistreach, agus tháinig sí ina céad amharclann fóirdheonaithe stáit i dtíortha an Bhéarla. Coinníonn ar An Chomhairle Ealaíon, mar aon lenár gcuid cairde ár bpatrúin agus sibhse, ár lucht féachana, tacaíocht a thabhairt dár gcuid oibre.

I 1951, rinneadh damáiste do bhunfhoirgnimh Amharclann na Mainistreach de bharr dóiteáin. Athlonnaíodh Amharclann na Mainistreach go dtí Amharclann na Banríona. Cuig bliana déag cothrom an lae sin anonn, ar an 18 Iúil 1966, bhog Amharclann na Mainistreach foirgneamh nua, a dhear Michael Scott, ar an láthair chéanna.

I Meán Fómhair 2006 d'fhógair an Rialtas go mbeadh comórtas dearaidh idirnáisiúnta ar siúl chun ionad buan nua a chruthú d'Amharclann na Mainistreach, a bheidh suite ar Ché Sheoirse i mBaile Átha Cliath. I Ndeireadh Fómhair 2007 fógraíodh an coiste moltóireachta don chomórtas.

Idir an dá linn, thugamar faoi chlár athchóirithe agus uasghrádaithe d'fhonn cur leis an eispéireas dár gcuid ealaíontóirí agus daoibhse, a lucht féachana. Chuimsigh sé seo an t-athchumrú radacach, ar cuireadh fáilte fhorleathan roimhe, in halla éisteachta Amharclann na Mainistreach.

Go raibh maith agaibh as bheith linn don léiriú seo. Tá súil againn go mbainfidh sibh taitneamh as an seó agus tá súil againn nach fada eile arís go mbeidh sibh inár gcuideachta in Amharclann na Mainistreach.

Creative Team

DAVID LEVEAUX
DIRECTOR

DAVID PREVIOUSLY DIRECTED *Three Sisters* at the Abbey Theatre. Recent productions in London include Tom Stoppard's *Arcadia*. Broadway productions include *Cyrano de Bergerac* with Kevin Kline, *The Glass Menagerie* with Jessica Lange, *Fiddler on the Roof*, Tom Stoppard's *Jumpers* (Tony Award nomination for Outstanding Direction), *Nine* with Antonio Banderas (Tony Award for Best Revival and nomination for Outstanding Direction), Stoppard's *The Real Thing* (Tony Award for Best Revival), Harold Pinter's *Betrayal* with Juliette Binoche, *Electra* with Zoë Wanamaker (Tony Award nomination), Eugene O'Neill's *Anna Christie* with Liam Neeson and Natasha Richardson (Tony Award for Best Revival) and *A Moon for the Misbegotten* with Kate Nelligan (Tony Award nomination for Outstanding Direction). Other productions include *Jumpers* (West End, London), *The Real Thing, Electra* (Donmar Warehouse), Harold Pinter's *No Man's Land* and *Moonlight* with Harold Pinter and Ian Holm, *Betrayal*, Neil LaBute's *The Distance from Here* (Almeida Theatre), *Jumpers, The Father* (National Theatre, London), *'Tis Pity She's a Whore, Romeo and Juliet* (RSC) and *A Moon for the Misbegotten*, for which he received a Society of West End Theatre Award (Riverside Studios). Opera includes *The Turn of the Screw* (Scottish Opera, Tramway), *The Marriage of Figaro* and Strauss's *Salomé* (English National Opera). In 1993, he formed Theatre Project Tokyo, an independent theatre company with executive producer Hitoshi Kadoi.

MIKE BRITTON
SET AND COSTUME DESIGN

MIKE PREVIOUSLY DESIGNED set and costumes for *Three Sisters* at the Abbey Theatre. Other recent design work includes *Statement of Regret* (National Theatre, London), *The Winter's Tale, Pericles, Madness in Valencia* (RSC), *The Vertical Hour* (Royal Court), *That Face* (Royal Court Upstairs/Duke of Yorks), *A Midsummer Night's Dream, Antony and Cleopatra, Coriolanus* (Shakespeare's Globe), *Period of Adjustment* (Almeida), *Walk Hard* (Tricycle), *Pure Gold* (Soho Theatre), *Nakamitsu* (The Gate, London), *Glass Eels, Comfort Me With Apples* (Hampstead Theatre), *Henry V*, Manchester Evening Post Award for Best Design, *Mirandolina* (Royal Exchange, Manchester), *Wuthering Heights, The Lady from the Sea*, TMA Award for Best Design, *She Stoops to Conquer* (Birmingham Rep), *People at Sea* (Salisbury Playhouse), *The Hypochondriac, Noises Off, Dr Faustus* (Liverpool Playhouse), *The Morris* (Liverpool Everyman), *Don't Look Now* (Sheffield Lyceum, Lyric Hammersmith), *Twelfth Night* (Theatre Royal, Plymouth), *John Bull's Other Island* (Lyric Theatre, Belfast), *The Comedy of Errors, Bird Calls* (Crucible, Sheffield), *Tartuffe, The Gentlemen from Olmedo, The Venetian Twins, The Triumph of Love, Dancing at Lughnasa* (Watermill, Newbury), *The Age of Consent* (Pleasance Edinburgh/Bush Theatre) and *Rudolf* (a musical for Vereinigte Buhnen Wien at the Raimund Theatre, Vienna).

MATTHEW RICHARDSON
LIGHTING DESIGN

MATTHEW RECENTLY DESIGNED the lighting for *Only an Apple* at the Abbey Theatre. Other lighting designs include *A Midsummer Night's Dream, Hamlet, The Park, The Cordelia Dream* (RSC), *Six Characters Looking for an Author, Doctor Faustus, Hobson's Choice* (Young Vic), *The Birthday Party* and *Nine Plays and a Recipe* (Citizens Theatre, Glasgow). Opera lighting designs include *Otello, Macbeth* (La Scala, Milan), *Eugene Onegin, Lulu* (Glyndebourne), *Fidelio, From the House of the Dead, Pelleas and Melisande* (ENO), *Cherubin, Falstaff* (Royal Opera House), *A Midsummer Night's Dream, Moses and Aron* (Metropolitan Opera, New York), *Don Carlos, Julietta, Peter Grimes* (Paris Opera), *Les Troyens* (Munich Opera), *Jenufa* and *Mefistofele* (Netherlands Opera). Work as a director includes *Macbeth* (Malmö Opera, Sweden), *Rigoletto, Boris Godunov* (New Zealand Opera), *The Cunning Little Vixen, Turandot* (Norrlands Opera, Sweden) and *The Marriage of Figaro* (BBC Television).

CORIN BUCKERIDGE
COMPOSER

THIS IS CORIN'S FIRST TIME working at the Abbey Theatre. He was Musical Associate at Chichester Festival Theatre from 1987 to 1989. Composition work includes *Our Lady of Sligo* (National Theatre, London), *Jumpers* (National Theatre and Broadway), *King John, 'Tis Pity She's*

a Whore, King Baby, Transit of Venus, The Merchant of Venice, Richard III, A Warwickshire Testimony (RSC), *Twelfth Night* (Regent's Park), *The Three Musketeers* (Bristol Old Vic) and many productions for Leicester Haymarket, Coventry Belgrade, West Yorkshire Playhouse, English Touring Theatre and the West End, including *Arcadia*. Music for short films includes *It's All Happening!, Ingrid Knows Best* and *Catching the Moon*. He provided the arrangements for Ian Bostridge's *The Noel Coward Songbook* for EMI. Work as Musical Director includes *The Taming of the Shrew*, music by Stephen Warbeck, *The Jovial Crew*, music by Ian Dury and Mickey Gallagher (RSC), *Marianne Dreams*, music by Paul Englishby (Almeida) and the European and Japanese tours of *Fosse*. He was supervising Music Director for the Italian and South African productions of *Chicago*, for which he was also MD in London. He is currently Musical Director for the West End production of *Hairspray*. He lives in London with his wife and three children.

BEN DELANEY
SOUND DESIGN

BEN WORKED AS SOUND DESIGNER on *The Last Days of a Reluctant Tyrant* at the Abbey Theatre. He graduated from Trinity College Dublin in 2007 with a Masters in Music and Media Technology, specialising in surround sound mixing and digital art. He is a composer of electronic music and found sound. Ben is currently in-house sound engineer at the Abbey Theatre.

DICK STRAKER
VIDEO DESIGN

THIS IS DICK'S FIRST TIME working at the Abbey Theatre. He formed Mesmer to provide projection design and image production services for theatre, performance and visual arts. His collaboration with directors, photographers, choreographers and artists has resulted in a wide range of achievement at the forefront of new forms of image presentation. Recent designs include *The Mountaintop* (about Martin Luther King), *The Guardians* (a High Tide festival production) and *Just Add Water* (Shobana Jeyasingh Dance Company at The Linbury). Previous designs include *Rushes*, a new ballet and Wagner's *Ring Cycle* (Royal Opera House), four Alexander McQueen fashion shows, *Orlando* (Sadler's Wells), *Sugar Mummies* (Royal Court), *The Woman in White*, (London and New York), *Julius Caesar* (Barbican Theatre), *Richard II*, (Old Vic) and *Henry V* (National Theatre, London).

BRENDAN GUNN
DIALECT COACH

BRENDAN LAST WORKED at the Abbey Theatre on *Ages of the Moon* and *Kicking a Dead Horse*. Other recent theatre credits include *Faith Healer* (Gate Theatre), *Antigone* (Primecut), *Dancing at Lughnasa*, *Be My Baby* and *The Homeplace* (Lyric Theatre, Belfast). His many film and television credits include *The Long Walk, Triage, A Shine of Rainbows, Cherry Bomb, Ghost Machine, The Return, Sweeney Todd, PS I Love You, Damage, The Painted Veil, Middletown, The Illusionist, Last Holiday, Breakfast on Pluto, Tara Road, The Mighty Celt, Inside I'm Dancing, Man About Dog, Veronica Guerin, Song for a Raggy Boy, Evelyn, Buffalo Soldiers, Meet Joe Black, This is My Father, The Boxer, The Butcher Boy, Michael Collins, Nothing Personal, Circle of Friends, Widows' Peak, In the Name of the Father, Into the West, December Bride* and *The Lonely Passion of Judith Hearne*.

SOPHIE MOTLEY
RESIDENT ASSISTANT DIRECTOR

SOPHIE WAS RECENTLY APPOINTED Resident Assistant Director at the Abbey Theatre. She was Assistant Director on *The Rivals* directed by Patrick Mason (Abbey Theatre). She is a graduate of the Samuel Beckett Centre. She trained on Rough Magic's SEEDS programme and the National Theatre Studio's directing course. Directing credits include *Corners* (ANU), *Extremities* (Spark to a Flame), *Invisible Atom* (ShinyRedChocolatePaper), *The Water Harvest* (Prime Cut), *Autobahn* (DYT), *The Gleaming Dark* (Old Vic), *Pilgrims of the Night* (Rough Magic SEEDS III) and *The Pitchfork Disney* (ShinyRedChocolatePaper, DU Players). She has worked as Assistant Director with Chichester Festival Theatre, The Gate, Rough Magic, Talking Birds and Pentabus. She recently formed ANU Productions.

Cast

DERBHLE CROTTY
TANIA

DERBHLE'S WORK AT THE ABBEY
theatre includes *Marble, An Ideal
Husband, Three Sisters, A Month in
the Country, The Dandy Dolls, Beauty
in a Broken Place, The Plough and the
Stars, Bailegangaire, Portia Coughlan*
(Royal Court co-production), *The Well
of the Saints* (Edinburgh Festival and
Perth), *The Mai* and *Katie Roche*. Other
theatre credits include *The Playboy of
the Western World, Sive, Gaslight, The
Good Father* (Druid), *The Home Place,
Dancing at Lughnasa* (Gate Theatre),
Everyday, Cat on a Hot Tin Roof
(The Corn Exchange), *The Playboy of
the Western World, Summerfolk, The
Merchant of Venice* (National Theatre,
London), *Alice Trilogy, The Weir*
(Royal Court), *Macbeth, Macbett, The
Penelopiad, I'll be the Devil, Little Eyolf,
Camino Real, Hamlet* (RSC), *Playing
the Wife* (Chichester), *Royal Supreme*
(Plymouth), *Miss Julie, Sandra/Manon*
(Vesuvius) and *Measure for Measure*
(Galloglass). Film and television credits
include *Notes on a Scandal, Inside I'm
Dancing, The Merchant of Venice, The
Clinic, Poorhouse, Gold in the Streets,
Samhain* and *Any Time Now*. Radio
includes *Myrrha, The Weight of Water,
St Patrick's Daughter* (BBC), *Quinn,
Bailegangaire, Portia Coughlan, The
Gospels of Aughamore* and *King Lear*
(RTÉ). Derbhle trained at the Samuel
Beckett Centre, Trinity College Dublin.

DESSIE GALLAGHER
ANDREW

THIS IS DESSIE'S FIRST TIME working
at the Abbey Theatre. His theatre
credits include *Macbecks* (Olympia,
Cork Opera House), *I Keano* (Olympia,
Cork Opera House, Lowry Theatre),
Alone It Stands (Duchess Theatre,
London), *Women on the Verge of HRT*
(Gaiety Theatre, Vaudeville Theatre,
London, Pavilion, Glasgow), *As
the Beast Sleeps* (Tricycle Theatre),
Dancing at Lughnasa, Hey Get a Life
(Andrew's Lane), *Translations* (Civic
Theatre and tour), *Out of Order Sweetie*
(Andrew's Lane and Tivoli Theatre)
and *The Importance of Being Earnest*
(Balor Theatre). Film and television
credits include *Val Falvey TD, The
Race, Occupation, Fifty Dead Men
Walking, Radio Garda, Jinx, The Eejits,
Showbands, Give My Head Peace, Love
is the Drug, Killinascully, King Arthur,
Reign of Fire, Ballykissangel, The
Closer You Get* and *The Breakfast*.

LISA HOGG
GIRL

THIS IS LISA'S FIRST TIME working at
the Abbey Theatre. Previous theatre
credits include *Dallas Sweetman*
(Paines Plough), *Loyal Women* (Royal
Court), *24 Hour Plays: Begin Again*
(Old Vic), *Waxing and Waning /
Tarmacking the Belt* (Soho Theatre /
Theatre Works), *Much Ado About
Nothing* (Stafford Festival), *Pete and
Me* (New End Theatre), *Many Loves*
(Lilian Baylis Theatre), *In the Jungle
of the City* (Windsor Arts Centre),

War Crimes Tribunal (Soho Theatre), *The Fisher King* and *War of Words* (Lyric Theatre Belfast). Television credits include Michelle in *Wuking the Dead*, Carol Best in *Best: His Mother's Son*, *Casualty* (BBC), Moira in *The Royal* (Yorkshire TV), *Trial and Retribution*, *The Commander* (La Plante Productions), *Wire in the Blood* (Coastal Productions), *Fallen* (Fremantle/Thames), *The Bill* (Talkback/Thames) and *Brookside* (Mersey TV). Films include Julie Taymor's *Across the Universe* (Revolution / Sony) and Yousaf Ali Khan's *Almost Adult*. Radio includes *Loyal Women* (BBC World Service).

recent theatre work includes *Handel's Crossing* (Fishamble) and *The Cripple of Inishmaan* with Druid and Atlantic Theatres for which he received an Irish Times Theatre Award Nomination for Best Actor and won an OBIE Award for Outstanding Performance and a Lucille Lortel Award for Best Actor. Television and film credits include *Little Foxes, Ella Enchanted, Deep Breaths, The Last Furlong, Speed Dating, Hide and Seek, The Deep End* and *LSD:73*. Aaron trained at the Samuel Beckett Centre, Trinity College and the British American Drama Academy, Oxford University. He is a founding member of Livin Dred Theatre Company.

AARON MONAGHAN
EVANS

AARON'S WORK AT THE ABBEY THEATRE includes *Romeo and Juliet, Drama at Inish, The Shaughraun* (Irish Times Theatre Award Nomination Best Supporting Actor), *Finders Keepers, The Burial at Thebes, I Do Not Like Thee Doctor Fell, The Wolf of Winter* and *She Stoops to Conquer* (Irish Times Theatre Award Nomination for Best Supporting Actor). Work with Druid includes *DruidSynge* (Galway, Dublin, Edinburgh International Festival, Inis Meain, New York, Guthrie Theater, Minneapolis), *Empress of India* (Dublin Theatre Festival), *The Walworth Farce, The Year of the Hiker* and *The Playboy of the Western World* (Ireland, England, Perth, Tokyo). Other theatre work includes *Alone it Stands* (Ireland, England, Malaysia), *Pubu* (Articulate Anatomy), *Roberto Zucco* (Bedrock Productions) and *The Tinker's Curse* (Livin Dred). His most

STEPHEN REA
NICHOLAS

STEPHEN BEGAN HIS CAREER at the Abbey Theatre before moving to London. His most recent appearances at the Abbey were in *Ages of the Moon* and *Kicking a Dead Horse* by Sam Shepard (also in New York and London). He was first directed by Sam Shepard in *Geography of a Horse Dreamer* at the Royal Court. He also acted in *Action* at the Royal Court and *Buried Child* and *Killer's Head* at the Hampstead Theatre and directed *Little Ocean* by Sam Shepard (also at the Hampstead). His first theatre role in London was as Tommy Owens in *The Shadow of a Gunman* with Jack McGowran at the Mermaid Theatre. He worked extensively at the National Theatre and the Royal Court where he worked with Samuel Beckett on *Endgame*. He was a founder member of Field Day Theatre Company with Brian Friel. Films include *Nothing*

*Personal, Ondine, Stuck, Sisters,
Sixty Six, Till Death, V for Vendetta,
Breakfast on Pluto, The River Queen,
The Good Shepherd, Control, The Halo
Effect, Ulysses, The I Inside, Evelyn,
FearDotCom, The Musketeer, The End
of the Affair, Guinevere, Still Crazy,
In Dreams, The Butcher Boy, Fever
Pitch, The Last of the High Kings,
Trojan Eddie, Michael Collins, The
Devil and the Deep Blue Sea, All Men
Are Mortal, Prêt a Porter, Interview
with a Vampire, Princess Caraboo,
Angie, Bad Behaviour, The Crying
Game, Life is Sweet, The Doctor and
the Devils, The House, The Company of
Wolves, Loose Connections* and *Angel.*
Stephen received an Oscar nomination
and a Golden Globe nomination for
The Crying Game and a Tony Award
nomination for *Someone Who'll Watch
Over Me.* Stephen is an Associate Artist
of the Abbey Theatre.

Abbey Theatre Supporters

Department of Arts, Sport and Tourism
An Roinn Ealaíon Spóirt agus Turasóireachta

The Abbey Theatre is funded by the
Arts Council/An Chomhairle Ealaíon
and receives financial assistance from
the Department of Arts, Sport and
Tourism.

*The Abbey Theatre is grateful to all
its sponsors, corporate members,
platinum patrons, patrons, friends
and donors for their generous support.*

SPONSORS

Anglo Irish Bank
CityJet
RTÉ
The Westin Dublin

CORPORATE MEMBERS

An Post
Behaviour & Attitudes
Irish Life & Permanent Plc
SIPTU
Sunday Business Post

PLATINUM PATRONS

Terry Calvani & Sarah Hill Calvani
Lilian & Robert Chambers
Conway Communications
Diageo Ireland
The Flowing Tide
Leonie Forbes
James McNally
Larry & Alice Mullen
Carmel Naughton
Vincent O'Doherty
Alan O'Sullivan
Andrew & Delyth Parkes

*Writer-in-Association
with the Abbey Theatre*

Phillip McMahon

Sponsored by

Anglo Irish Bank

PATRONS

Shaun & Sharon Brewster
Joe Byrne
Zita Byrne
Patricia Callan
John & Lara Cashman
Clarion Consulting
Gerald Clarke
Denis Cremins
Alf & Oonagh Desire
Donal & Caitríona
   Donnelly
John & Aoibheann
   Donnelly
Ian Donnelly
Michael Fadian & Dervila
   Layden
Gerard Kelly & Co Ltd
   Builders Providers
Jim Hender
Lanigan's Plough
Paul Leahy
Eugene Magee
Tom & Therese Martin
Sean & Maureen
   McCormack
Katia Meleady
David Mellon
Mindshare
McCullough Mulvin
   Architects
Caroline O'Donoghue
Tara O'Sullivan
Valerie O'Toole
Paul Rossiter
Matt Toomey
Lesley Wallace
Brian Walsh

JOINT FRIENDS

Edward & Helen Dowling
Silvia Gomez Giraldo &
   Mark Kavanagh
Michael & Fiona Lang
Tom & Mary O'Brien
Patrick Molloy & Nuala
   O'Donovan
Joe & Joan O'Toole
Stephanie Regan-Scott &
   Liam Scott

FRIENDS

John Allen
Gayle Bowen
Shelagh Brady
Frances Britton
Tony Brown
Adrian Burke
Eimear Burke
Fiona Butterfield
Ciaran Byrden
Margaret Cagney
Rory Campbell
Marie Carney
Clive Carroll
Mona Carton
Damien & Ann Comiskey
Martin Craul
Denise Cremins
Maureen Cunnane
Linda Curran
Thomas Curran
Paul Donnelly & Anna
   Pachi
Thomas Dooley
Thomas Dooley
Mary Rose Doorly
Thelma Doran
Declan Downs
Larry Doyle
Eleanor Ewings
Lucy Fallon-Byrne
Caoimhe Frain
Patrick Frain
Tony & Catherine
   Gillhawley
Myriam Gordon
Jack Griffin
Paul & Sheila Grimes
Ken Halpin
Sean & Mary Holahan
Susie Horn
Roger Hussey
Anthony Hyland
Noreen Hynes
Gary Joyce
Rachel Joyce
Claire Kehoe
Dara Kelleher
John Kelly
John King
Maire King

Steven Knowlton
James & Elizabeth Lally
Gabrielle Lynch
Sine Lynch
Mary Mac Aodha
Berna Mc Menamin
John McAuley
Mairead McCann
Raymond McCarthy
Teresa McColgan
Joseph McCullough
Mel McGrath
Brian Merriman & Aideen
   Rickard
Pat Monahan
Breege Murphy
John Murphy
Maria Murphy
Raoine Ni Iarnain
Deirdre Nolan
Senator David Norris
David O'Brien
Geraldine O'Brien
Hildegarde O'Connor
Mags Ó Dálaigh
Laurie O'Driscoll
Tom O'Gorman
Katherine O'Loughlin-
   Kennedy
Michael O'Mahony
Karen O'Shea
Denis & Marie O'Sullivan
David Parkes
Ruth Parkin
John Reynolds
Tony Ryan
Marcella Senior
Vincent Slattery
Ailbhe Smyths
Janette Stokes
Dr Mark Sugrue
Jean Tobin
Angela Tonge
Maureen Tyrrell
Ciaran Walsh
Janice Walsh
Nora Walsh
Philip Walshe
Róisín Weldon
Carol Wright

NEXT AT THE
ABBEY THEATRE

[BACK BY POPULAR DEMAND]
TERMINUS
Written and Directed by Mark O'Rowe
The ordinary turns to extraordinary in this vivid play.
10 NOVEMBER – 5 DECEMBER 2009 *on the Peacock stage*

———

[BACK BY POPULAR DEMAND]
AGES OF THE MOON
by Sam Shepard
A gruffly poignant and darkly funny play.
13 – 28 NOVEMBER 2009 *on the Abbey stage*

———

[BACK BY POPULAR DEMAND]
THE SEAFARER
Written and Directed by Conor McPherson
A thrilling tale of a debt with the Devil.
4 DECEMBER 2009 – 30 JANUARY 2010 *on the Abbey stage*

———

LITTLE GEM
by Elaine Murphy
A heart-warming tale of courage, comedy and romance.
19 JANUARY – 27 FEBRUARY 2010 *on the Peacock stage*

———

CHRIST DELIVER US!
by Thomas Kilroy
An emotionally compelling story about a generation of young people
who strive to understand their world.
— AN ABBEY THEATRE COMMISSION —

9 FEBRUARY – 13 MARCH 2010 *on the Abbey stage*

*Tickets from €15. For more information visit **www.abbeytheatre.ie***
*or call Box Office **(01) 87 87 222***

Sebastian Barry
Tales of Ballycumber

faber and faber

First published in 2009
by Faber and Faber Limited
74–77 Great Russell Street
London WC1B 3DA

Typeset by Country Setting, Kingsdown, Kent CT14 8ES
Printed in England by CPI Bookmarque, Croydon, Surrey

A CIP record for this book
is available from the British Library

978-0-571-25131-5

2 4 6 8 10 9 7 5 3 1

For Ellen
loved by all

Characters

Nicholas
a farmer

Evans
his young friend

Andrew
Evans's father

Tania
Nicholas's sister

A Girl

TALES OF BALLYCUMBER

SCENE ONE

Everything in place, but darkened. Downstage is a girl about thirteen or older, in a woollen hat and ordinary clothes, and she sings 'Heartbreak Hotel' by Elvis Presley in her own Wicklow accent. Then light away, and:

Nicholas is a dark-haired dark-faced, farmer of possibly Cromwellian stock; he could be mid-forties or fifty, hard to say. He wears clothes with no regard at all for anything except their nearness to hand and their usefulness. But he is shaven and fairly clean. He speaks with a Wicklow accent of the district around Tinahely. He is in principle well off, in that he owns the farm he works (perhaps he is the farm). But he left school at leaving-certificate level and is not much concerned with books. He needs glasses to read, but mostly for labels and suchlike to do with his farming. He has both sheep and cattle, mainly the latter. His farm is about a hundred acres, mostly steep ground and much of it ranged along the fringe of the frostline. In his youth he was a well-liked sportsman, but is more isolated now. He has no wife. The nearest neighbour is across the boggy land below, the Staffords. His own family is called Farquhar and has been in Ireland since the sixteenth century, although perhaps Nicholas himself is no longer aware of that.

Music. On the cyc: the neglected garden of the house. It is a promising day in spring outside; the daffodils, planted fifty years ago when his mother was young, are freshly open.

But he is on his knees before the fireplace – a good chimneypiece, but very chipped and worn.

9

In the room the only picture is an old framed photograph of John F. Kennedy.

Nicholas might be praying, but in fact he is waiting. There is a thumping sound somewhere high above him. Then a deluge of twigs and other dust and dirt arrives in the grate. Nicholas lets out a cry of success, reaches for a roll of black plastic bags, starts to stuff the debris into one. He is laughing as he does it.

The last thing he does is stick an old black kettle back on to a hook in the fireplace.

Nicholas Can't be doing without that.

> *Evans Stafford comes in; he is also laughing. He sits in the well-scooped-out chair by the fire, looking very comfortable. He is about seventeen maybe, a small, thin young man.*

So I was coming up the hill by the short field, and trying to take a peek up onto the upper garden where I have put the lambs, keeping an eye out for Mr Renard you may be certain, not thinking of anything at all, when I seen those two jackdaws working away, taking advantage of the nice weather. And flinging their damn twigs down the chimney and every scrap of sheep's wool they can find in the wires, and they couldn't a' had more than three days for the work, because I had fire in the fire Friday just, but that's all they needed, and a big crown of twigs then and muck, and then I seen you coming up along the ridge of the hill, I suppose you are going to Tinahely by the mountain, and I'm calling you then, and now we have done that job, let's have a little scald of our tea.

> *Nicholas pulls tea into two mugs – he has a plastic kettle on the table. His cup is an Elvis souvenir. He fetches a Club Milk out of the table drawer, and half-fecks it towards Evans.*

Evans Top job. They're late at their nest-building anyhow.

Nicholas Oh, it's second goes for them you can be sure. White, yellow, blue, snowdrop, daffodil and bluebell, and the birds that go with them, and the jackdaw goes with the yellow flowers at the very least. You might hear one walking on the roof at snowdrop time either.

Evans There must be a gazette in nature somewhere somehow, which the animals are reading carefully, isn't that it, Nicholas?

Nicholas They seem to know anyhow, however it is done. And the rooks, sure aren't they much worse. They're fighting in the beech trees over the best nests, and God only knows are they fighting husband and wife also, since they are wed to just the one ould bird all their lives, what sort of life is that for them, and then when the chicks are in, there's more just terrible caterwauling, and you don't get a hint of peace up there till May Day, by God. Such a racket was never heard in Christendom.

Evans And they're all yellow boys too, are they?

Nicholas When the first daffodil opens out there on the ould avenue, that my mother planted when she was a young wife come in here from Leitrim, the poor woman, that seems to spark them rooks. And you might go out to the grass there, as idle as you like, and see some poor ould remnant of a rook lying there, dead as a doornail, looking for all the world like a rector in his black suit. So death first, a taste of it, and then, all that argy-bargy over nests. And I wouldn't mind but their favourite tree is not a beech tree at all, but that ould sycamore, and they often say a bird knows the general health of a tree, so I suppose I am to imagine that the beech trees will be coming down on my head in the next unnatural and barbarous storm.

Evans They've stood this long.

Nicholas But sure everything has its term. As long as when they fall over they fall over into the upper garden, and don't be rattling our slates, which are already in a state, as you may have noticed.

Evans I did see a few slipped down, right enough.

Nicholas Sure the rain drips down on me in my bed upstairs. I keep moving the bed but the drips follow me.

Evans You may get someone to go about the roof in the summertime and solidify the whole thing.

Nicholas I may, and there are men asking two hundred euro a day for that work, and making worse damage clambering about.

Silence for a while.

Evans (*spotting the nature of Nicholas's mug*) I did have news for you. I was going to tell you first thing.

Nicholas What's that then, what's the news?

Evans (*counting them off on his fingers*) Elvis's great-great-great-great-grandfather was born in Hacketstown.

A few moments.

Nicholas By Jesus. That's news.

Evans I was reading it in the *Nationalist*. He was run out too. I don't know what he done. There were Mahers involved.

Nicholas Well, no change there.

Evans The Presleys had a house under Eagle Hill, which is a bare place enough still. Maybe he wasn't so hard to go.

Nicholas Jesus, I'd say you're right. These fucking bald hills. 'Let ye all go on to be helled,' says he, I'd say, and off he went.

Evans So himself and his brother up sticks and go to New Orleans. And he married a girl, and the son out of that married, and the son out of that, and then I think we get to Elvis's father, and then Elvis. So.

Nicholas Well, if that don't beat all. If you live long enough you'll have everything explained to you. There am I all these years rejoicing in the music of Elvis and now I know why it knocks me to the marrow. Now I know. And it was you told me.

Evans I meant to say it the second I was in the door, but the chimney thing put it out of my head.

Nicholas Fair dues.

Silence again for a while.

Evans So, up at the Medlands dance the other night, she was there, you know, Patsy Byrne, the girl I told you about, and I was over to her asking her to dance, she was looking like gold she was, all in this lovely blue dress, you would hardly dare to look at her, and she turns her face to me, with those greeny-blue eyes she has, I never saw eyes like them before, it's probably a sort of wrong thing in the DNA, if she was a beast you might worry about it, but eyes like that in a girl, it makes your bladder go weak on you some way. But I can't dance tonight, she says, I can't, there's been a tragedy, and I'm only here to be with my girlfriends, she says, or else I may go mad at home. So I says, what's all that about, and she says, didn't you hear, Evans, no, I says, and she says, well, Michael is after being found hanged in the bathroom with his school tie, that's her brother Michael, who's in transition year he was, no pressure on him that anyone knew of, sure it's a big doss year isn't it, but supposedly he came home one night, gave his mother a kiss, and went up to the loo, and snagged the tie around the strong nail that was there to hold a mirror, and somehow got his body onto it, and do you know, his legs were trailing on the ground, he hadn't even made a move to save himself, as you might expect. So I says to Patsy, I am terrible sorry to hear that, Patsy, and she says, thank you, Evans, like a person at a funeral, and everyone around going mad at the dance, some ould Eminem song it was.

Nicholas I remember you telling me about her right enough. I remember you saying about the green eyes.

Evans Greeny-blue.

Nicholas Update. Greeny-blue. So Byrne. So she's with the other crowd?

Evans Hey?

Nicholas She's a Catholic.

Evans I suppose.

Nicholas Now you couldn't be trusting a girl like that to look after you.

Evans Hey?

Nicholas I'm not saying she'll be all bad, but you can't trust a Catholic person, ah, you can have a drink with them, why not, sociable like, I've nothing against them, but you couldn't trust a girl like that to love you proper, no. If you ask a Catholic carpenter to cut you a piece of wood, he'll cut it short and charge the extra inch, and then the bloody plank will fall off the ceiling for want of proper length. Even Catholic businesses like to have a Protestant accountant, because you can't trust a Catholic, that's all.

Evans You think so?

Nicholas That's what I hear about it.

Evans If you saw her eyes you wouldn't be caring about that.

Nicholas That's very sad about the brother though, yes. You do hear about things like that now all over Wicklow. Young people. What is it about life now that makes them want to leave it? And there was that young lass over the other side of Ballycumber, that had the cancer, and she was only eleven, such a fine brave little lass, and went through two years of hope and hell, and then the poor parents burying her, and all the parish ranged about the grave, looking like they had come through a great storm of wind, and the grief of the parents such as like would haunt your dreams forever, a girl that loved life and wanted to live it, and then you have a fella like your friend's brother, as healthy as a lamb I will not doubt, and electing to remove himself, and causing no doubt the same mountain of sorrow to his parents, and the parish ranged again, and I don't know, but there is a terrible necklace of grief in all that. That same night she was buried, the little lass I mean, one of the most beautiful wee girls that was ever seen around Ballycumber, a pearl among children she was, and they put her into the churchyard a few miles from her home, and I was passing it that very same night in my car, coming back from Aughrim with a few messages, and I don't know, but I got this terrible strange feeling that she was sitting in the back of the car, in the darkness there, not saying a word, and I was so afraid to glance into the mirror, in case I would see that pretty face, and I knew well she was there, and I knew it was because my road home would take me past her parents, and she would have been wondering what she was doing so far from home, and in the darkness, and seen me passing, and took a lift, and you know I was terrified, my blood was running chill in my veins like a January rain, but I thought, I will do well to bring my neighbour's child home, I would not leave her there for all the world in the darkness, I would not. And when I passed her mother's house, I sort of felt she was gone, and I wasn't frightened then so much as glad.

Evans I remember that. Everyone loved her right enough. She was a great girl. Didn't she want to be a rally driver or something?

Nicholas She did. She was ambitious right enough in that direction. That was an affliction visited on her mother and father. But it came to them all natural and nothing to be done in the end only love her, adore her. But your friend's brother, how could he do that, and the terrible awful dark grief given to his family?

Evans He wouldn't have known that maybe.

Nicholas Ah yes. At that age, you think if you kill yourself on a Monday, you can get up on Tuesday just the same as always. You think sure you'll live for ever, and nothing can hurt you, even death. But. It's old as hills maybe. Yonder song of Elvis's, 'Heartbreak Hotel', was wrote about a fella took his life in a hotel in Memphis years ago. Folded his clothes on the chair as neat as you like, and left a note, 'I walk a lonely road.'

Silence for a while.

Evans Anyway, Nicholas, I would be trusting her.

Nicholas Who?

Evans Patsy Byrne.

Nicholas You would be?

Evans Yes.

Nicholas Fair enough so.

Silence for a while.

Evans Beautiful eyes.

Nicholas Fair enough so.

Evans And did you see a fox then near the lambs?

Nicholas No, I did not. I saw only a kestrel hanging in the air to be kamikaze-ing down on the mice and the rabbits. I might go out in a while and have another look at them.

Evans I hear there were lambs lost to my uncle in Crossbridge, but he didn't know if it was foxes or dogs.

Nicholas Jesus, people have an awful queer lot of dogs these times.

Evans They do.

Nicholas They're not happy till they have three dogs, and not sheepdogs even, but either great brutes of things, or little small yokes, you know. Though a sheepdog will kill lambs too, if it's allowed to roam. It's mostly sheepdogs do be killing sheep, which is strange enough. But what use is one of them little dogs, you tell me.

Silence for a little.

Evans Pomeranians.

Silence for a little.

Nicholas That's it.

Silence again.

Anyway, Evans, you want to be expanding out.

Evans What, Nicholas?

Nicholas You don't want to go attaching yourself to any lassie round here.

Evans Why not?

Nicholas A young fella needs to have a broad view of the world.

Evans Oh, yes?

Nicholas We're a little place here. Here now, listen, I'll tell you a tale, if you want.

Evans Well?

After a little while.

Nicholas Do you know, in the thirties, there were twenty families living up here on the mountain, that is to say, on the two sides of Ballycumber. But they all died off. In four or five years, just before the war, they all died off. There was a school there one time, full of children, and now it is empty, and all the little ruins you do see when you go about were the houses of families, stuffed with children. Old Protestants mostly, living poorly, but closely, and there it was. And the great catastrophe that struck those people, kin of your own many of them would have been, Evans, was TB – human TB, you know, it wasn't carried in by deer and badgers, no. And it burned through the people here like a gorse fire in February, eating away chap and grown person alike. And the why of that was, we were too numerous, close, and local. You want a broad view of the world. There were people that went out from here too, you know, that are forgotten now. One of them Laurences down in Moyne went off to the Crimean War, and was later setting up a great newspaper in America. And one time when the countess was still alive in Coollattin, this was the centre of the world for four hundred years, when the Fitzwilliams were in their years of power. We all came for them, you know, in bygone days. The Humes of Humewood, all those great people, and every one of them gone now. And I'll tell you another thing, Evans, just to illustrate my point to you. If you don't mind.

Evans Well, Nicholas.

Nicholas You know the old house there at Coollattin where they have the golf course now. Well, it's looked after by a fella called Seamus Byrne. He just goes in and makes sure the slates are good and what not. And just the other day, he has a request from someone to see the old place. So, he goes to the house to oblige this woman, and he shows her the house. Now you may know the legend of that place. The last countess turned day into night, drinking to while away the hours of her life. When she was a young woman her husband left her and took up with one of the lovely Kennedy girls. And the old man of the Kennedys, wasn't he Joe, he was, didn't want his daughter marrying a Protestant, so, the two of them, it was Kick was her name, wasn't that a funny name, and I don't recall the name of the Fitzwilliam man, but, anyway, Joe Kennedy was down in the warm part of France, so the couple took a plane down there to see him, to be asking his permission to marry, you know, and didn't the plane go down into the sea. And they were killed. And she was the first of Joe Kennedy's children to be killed. And Joe Junior then was killed in the war, and of course John F. and Bobby murdered, and the son of John F. gone down recent in his own plane, you know. Well, Seamus Byrne was showing this lady around. And he shows her the painted wallpaper in the drawing room and in the countess's bedroom, where she spent her last lonely years, well, all her years were lonely, but in her old age when she was fastened to her bed, and only cats for company, and, says Seamus, there was a strange chill in the room, and he suddenly got the feeling that whatever spirit of the countess remained, didn't want that other living woman there, he got this feeling as strong as a frost against his body, and who was that woman, Evans, only one of the surviving Kennedy girls, herself an old woman now, a sister of that very Kick Kennedy. And what impulse had brought her to see that house, what thought, what thought? And you can imagine how the old countess would have bridled to have her in her bedroom, the sister of the woman that had destroyed her life.

Silence for a bit.

That's very strange, I think. (*A moment.*) I'm not saying . . . The father brought yon portrait back, the time his nibs dipped home to Wexford.

Evans The thing is, Nicholas, I love that girl.

Nicholas What?

Evans I love her.

Nicholas You love her?

Evans Yes.

Nicholas But you never danced with her. (*A moment.*) I don't hold with these mixed dances. In my time when there was a social, you knew where you were. There never ever were a Catholic at our dances. My God, no. Because it was for us to be seeing the talent, and who we might fancy, you know?

Evans And how would you know, Nicholas?

Nicholas What?

Evans How would you know if someone was a Catholic?

Nicholas What?

Evans How could you tell?

Nicholas Jesus, sure, we'd do. You'd know straight away. One glance. Jesus.

Evans Well.

Nicholas We'd nothing against them, but we just didn't want to be marrying them. You know.

Evans And did you have a girl, Nicholas?

Nicholas What?

Evans Did you go out with anyone?

Nicholas I went out with lots. Lots. There was the pictures in Tinahely that time. *Viva Las Vegas*, hah? Elvis Presley indeed. I should of gone to see it in Hacketstown, hah? (*Singing, badly enough.*) 'Viva Las Vegas, viva Las Vegas.' I remember that. That was a good picture. We were all Elvises for a week after seeing that.

Evans You didn't marry though.

Nicholas Well, that's obvious.

Evans Why not?

Nicholas Well, the mother was here till only recent, and – (*A moment.*) Ah, Jaysus, did I want a woman around the place? I don't know. I'd no interest. My sister Tania hasn't given up hope, I am sure.

Evans Interest?

Nicholas Aye.

Evans You don't get lonely then, up here?

Nicholas Lonely? No. Sure I have the dogs. And the beasts. Sure I don't have time to be lonely. And I should be going out now like I said to look at the lambs. I should go out, and look at the lambs.

Evans You should go out and look at them.

Nicholas I should go out and look at the lambs.

Evans I'll be going off myself, I was only going up the mountain, I like to cross the mountain to Tinahely, by the old road. (*He checks his mobile phone. To himself.*) It's gone dead.

Nicholas It was the only road in the old days. You wouldn't have put a horse by the car road. Sure, that would be madness.

Evans Aye. I'll see you then, Nicholas.

Nicholas Aye, God bless.

Evans Thanks for the tea.

Nicholas Oh, Jesus. Thanks for the help with, you know. I couldn't a' done that on me own.

Evans So long.

Nicholas So long, now.

SCENE TWO

Music. The next day. Nicholas is on his knees again, knocking the ashes off the fire he has banked down the night before, and when the embers flare red he puts new turf on them. He is very happy in this work.

On the cyc, there is a fox moving across the upper field. The wide spread of the mountain.

The radio is going, with the early morning news show, but it's just a muddle of voices. It's another fine day outside, though there's a lock of ice around the house, and indeed inside it.

Nicholas is singing 'Viva Las Vegas' to himself and, inasmuch as he can, doing the old Elvis moves where he is on the hearth.

There is a banging on his front door so he goes out to it.

Nicholas (*off*) Ah, sure, Andrew, you never need to knock on my door, come straight in anytime.

Andrew I felt I should be knocking.

Andrew Stafford comes in with Nicholas. He's in his late fifties, a big, broad man. He is known for his gentleness though.

I'm not coming between you and a job of work?

Nicholas Not a bit of it, I was just getting the ould fire going. Evans helped with the ould nest was in it yesterday. He's a good boy. I think he's a grand boy, and a credit to you, Andrew. A child that can speak out good in grown-up company is a well-raised child.

Andrew He's no child really now.

Nicholas I think of him as just a chap, but of course he is not, you are right, Andrew, he is not. Please sit down there now the turf is blowing good.

Andrew No, Nicholas, I did not come to sit.

Nicholas Oh?

Andrew I came to tell you something and I came to ask you something.

He has a folded piece of paper in his right hand, that he is moving about in his fingers. But now he doesn't say anything for a moment.

God knows in the first moment it is like being shot through the heart.

Nicholas What is, Andrew?

Andrew Then it is like a man came out of the bushes at you with a bludgeon and bludgeoned you, and hit you again and again on the crown, and broke it, and then it feels like your brains are in the air, and there is an ache in them so great that even a cold, hard person must cry out.

Nicholas What, in the name of God?

Andrew And I may walk about the world now that we know, Nicholas, I may come up to you here in later times, maybe, and I may go down into Tinahely and get messages for Mags, God help her, I may go into Paddy for meat, I may go into Londis for other things, I may go to the show in August and watch the horses and the cattle, I may do a thousand things that I have always done, and taken great pleasure in them, but there won't be any pleasure in them now.

Nicholas Jesus, Andrew, please do sit down. Please, man dear.

Andrew does sit in the same chair where Evans sat.

What, man dear?

Andrew It was late yestreen and I was keeping an ear cocked for Evans coming home, the way you do in a house with only one son in it, and I saw the frost clamp down the fields as the light went out of things, and Mags was banging about in the kitchen boiling spuds or whatever it was, and I was standing in the good parlour because it has a view of the mountain walk, and thinking what a poor old faded show the chairs made, and I was hoping to see his figure coming back over Ballycumber, and I was thinking stupid thoughts, like I hope he brought his scarf, because there will be a cut in that night wind, and I was thinking what it is when a child grows bigger, and is not a child, as we were saying, and I was thinking of when he was a little chap there in the house, a bright little boy, playing the piano and us fetching him here and there for things, and how bright he was at his school.

Nicholas As you were yourself, Andrew.

Andrew That's a fact. And the nuns in Bunclody said he had brains to burn, and rightly so. And I was thinking of the softness of him, the littleness in his bed at night, when

I might go in to kiss him, and make sure there were no sounds that had disturbed him, so he could sleep soundly, as I think a child ought, and. Now why was I thinking old thoughts like that, standing in the parlour? I'm not a man to go back over things, I stare the morning in the face. But. And he didn't come home, and I rang his phone, adjudging that he would be in Murphy's having a pint with pals, and of course, you only ever get the answering message off his phone, does he ever have it on, I do not think so.

Nicholas Well.

Andrew One time some years ago he was at a dance in the Medlands, he was only thirteen, and he was to take the bus back to Tinahely, though I had dropped him to Bunclody, but the bus driver wanted the full fare from him, and he only had five euro, so he was put off, a chap of thirteen in that wild town as the pubs were closing.

Nicholas Barbarous.

Andrew And by a miracle he had money in his phone, and rang me, and how I did it I don't know, but I got from Ballycumber to Bunclody in about fifteen minutes, which is not possible in a car, but there it was, and I thanked God and all his angels that he had his phone working that time, I tremble to think what might have happened to him. So I was trying to ring him last night and then when it was past midnight I wished I had rang Murphy's to ask them was he there, and I hadn't thought of doing it, I don't know why, and you know how cold it was last night, it was a wonder the waterpipes survived it, ah, but, I told myself, he'll have stopped with friends, you know, as they do at that age, although I wanted to strangle him for not telling me. So me and Mags went to bed a bit awkward and concerned but, you know, thinking the best of the matter. Then bright early I rose up and it was still quite dark, and still cold, and the yard lights looked a little bleak the way they do, and nothing was stirring, though to be honest I saw a bloody rat walk down the yard as brazen as you like –

Nicholas Ho.

Andrew – and I went out and sort of sniffed the air, like I might be able to tell something from it. Like I might smell my son on it. And I gathered my old coats about me and put on this woollen hat and my working gloves and I started up the dark hill, thinking I would be sure to meet him on his way home. And as I came to your boundary stone there, and my feet came onto the frostline, it was just then the sun came up from behind Knockroe, pushing light onto the valley, and all the frost on the heather glittered back at it, as if some person had thrown a huge cloth across the hillside made of white stars, do you know, and in that moment I could fear nothing, because it is such a beautiful place kept here by God, and the stillness and the quietness, and I think even the old pagans felt that, and haven't they left enough old forts scattered about to show they favoured Ballycumber. And I came up to the boundary stone, with the figure of the woman on it.

Nicholas Aye.

Andrew A quare ould figure. And.

Andrew stares forward for a while.

It was then it felt like . . .

A few moments.

And I carried him down to the house. And.

Nicholas What do you mean?

Andrew Carried him, on my back.

Nicholas Why?

Andrew Because he was shot in the stomach.

26

Nicholas Evans is dead?

Andrew No, no. He's with his mother in the house. I came up here.

Nicholas Andrew, I'm so sorry you have had this happen. I cannot tell you how sorry I am. Who shot him?

Andrew He shot himself.

Nicholas Why would he do that?

Andrew That's what I want to ask you.

Nicholas Me? How in the world would I know?

Andrew When I came to him and saw the blood in his hands and the gun, he said, just like you now, 'I'm sorry, Dada,' and I knelt to him and looked at the blood, and I said, 'But Evans, why did you do this?' And he said, 'I don't know, but I have wrote it on a note in my pocket,' he said, and I fetched out the note from his pocket, and this is the note. And all it says is, 'Nicholas Farquhar knows.' So I thought before I would go entirely mad I might walk up here and ask you what it is you know.

Nicholas I know nothing. Show me the note. Where are my glasses? I can never find them.

Andrew Was he here with you yesterday?

Nicholas Yes, yes, I told you, he was sitting there exactly where you are sitting.

Andrew And you were speaking?

Nicholas (*finding his glasses, reading the note*) We were talking, passing the time, drinking our tea, this and that, just tales and talk.

Andrew draws the gun from his coat and puts it on his lap. Nicholas takes off the glasses again.

That's the gun?

27

Andrew That's it there. That's the gun we use for the dogs when they get old, and an injured ewe, or a beast with a broken leg. I keep it in the good parlour because no one goes in there. But he must have come back in the night and crept in there and got it, and maybe wrote his note, and then gone back up to the stone, and then –

Nicholas I think if you asked him what he meant he would not say anything bad about our talk.

Andrew He is not talking now. The carry down the hill weakened him so. I suppose it is a coma. I suppose Mags has Dr Snow called and soon he will be there. But, I saw wounds like that in the Congo when I served there in the fifties, stomach wounds, they are wounds that medics shake their heads at. I think he will die. I think my son will die. I think I would be happy to kill you, if you caused this, Nicholas.

Nicholas Set your mind at rest about that, Andrew. Nothing amiss was spoke. Do I even remember what we said? It was chatting, like we always do. He often is passing and he comes in and we are chatting. We are great friends. You should go back down, Andrew, it may be he is not so badly wounded, you should be with him.

Andrew You think so?

Nicholas I do, forgive me. You have suffered a shock so great you will see shadows and omens everywhere. Man dear, your suffering is great. There's no greater. I have no wife nor children, and I can feel it.

Andrew lifts the gun and points it at Nicholas.

Andrew You swear? You swear on your poor mother's life?

Nicholas I swear. If I thought I had said anything, I would be happy for you to shoot me. How could I live after that?

Andrew (*undoing the safety catch*) You are sure? You are certain, Nicholas?

Nicholas I am.

Andrew breaks down, lifting a hand to his face. Nicholas takes the gun from him and sets it on the hearth.

Go down this minute. Things may have improved. Dr Snow is a great expert, and think of all the shootings these times in Dublin, they may know their way around it, and you might be needed to go in an ambulance, Andrew, and Mags will need you.

Andrew I will go. I will.

Nicholas Let me bring you down.

Andrew No. I don't want you coming down there. I have his feelings to consider.

Nicholas Let me bring you to the door.

Andrew All right.

When he turns there is blood on his back. Nicholas's hand hesitates to touch it.

Nicholas It's a bit grubbied up your coat is.

Andrew sees the blood on Nicholas's hand.

Andrew He's been in scrapes before. I wish it was a scrape I would fix. When he was four, he loved to play on an ancient apple tree in the orchard. It was so old and slippery and even fallen over in a storm, but it still bore apples, so I left it. I left it and Evans loved to climb about it. It was only two feet off the ground, the length of the trunk. And he was playing there one day, and he must have slipped on the bark, and put out an arm to stop himself hitting the ground. And his arm was so soft and new, he broke it at the elbow.

Nicholas The boy.

Andrew I was shifting some stuff in a corner of the orchard and heard him mewling like a kitten, making this tiny sound. So I carried him into the house and Mags phoned for the ambulance in Tallaght, which is a long journey for them, and I sat the little man on my lap. I didn't dare move him again for fear of the bones sticking out under the skin. It looked like the four bones had parted at the elbow and the lower two had risen into the upper arm. So the ambulance comes and I get in just as we were, and sit there, and this lady is talking to me, and I don't know what it was, but I started to feel terrible car sick, maybe it was the shock, and yet I couldn't get her to stop chatting, and didn't like to try because they are so kind, those people. So halfway to Tallaght around Blessington I'm puking into a dish. And Evans as quiet as a cat.

Nicholas By God.

Andrew Then we come into the hospital and we're stuck together still like glue, and this little nurse comes up and she's Chinese maybe, and doesn't speak much English, but she wants to weigh him. She says she is honour bound to weigh him, so she can give the numbers to the fella giving the anaesthetic. And I couldn't get her to understand the little lad's arm was broken and it was only me holding him together, and there'd be a disaster if she moved him onto the scales, and him having to be standing up.

Nicholas I know.

Andrew So we were wrestling there, me and the nurse, with words anyhow. And then in the end of all I cried out, 'How much do you think he weighs? Have a guess,' you know, like it was one of them games on television. 'You have a guess,' I said, 'because I'm not handing him over,' and I didn't, no, I was that obstinate, till the trolley came for him and all. And then they put him back together. And a lovely job they did. Just like new again.

Suddenly, grabbing Nicholas by the lapels, despairing:

What did you say to him, you fucker?

Nicholas I never said nothing. I never said nothing.

Andrew drops his lapels gently enough. Nicholas helps Andrew out, a hand on his shoulder.

Andrew Now all the king's horses and all the king's men . . .

Nicholas goes back and sits in his chair with his back to the table. He is probably crying. There are glimmers of a young girl sitting under it, a little hunched like a hiding child.

Nicholas (*without looking round, fearfully enough*) Is that you, childeen?

Girl Yes, aye.

Nicholas I am in a great deal of trouble, a great deal of trouble.

Girl He loves his child is all it is.

Nicholas What is that?

Girl He loves his child, he loves him, he loves that Evans.

Nicholas He does of course. Of course that's it. He loves him. How he wended up here when his child was lying bleeding below I couldn't understand. But he was thinking, if I can find that lie in Nicholas Farquhar's gob, I can cure him, I can cure him. I can fetch it out, and break off a bit of it, and cure him, like the doctor below might put discouragement against the flu, with a little jab of flu in the shape of the vaccine.

Girl That's it. You'd only know that if there was father enough in you. There must be a biteen of it in you.

Nicholas Well, I never seen no father worth talking about around here, unless it was Andrew, or your own father maybe.

Girl My own father is a hero to me.

Nicholas A bloody hero is what he is, that's what he is.

Girl He never let a minute work against me. Him and Mammy.

She begins to clear up a little for Nicholas, wiping the table as may be.

They never let a moment to be hurting me. And there might have been several to them. In out to the hospital they ferried me, and we were never doing much but laughing, day or night, and you know how the dark trees might be lowering a person in their mood, going past the ould car windows. He had seven all-Ireland champion hurlers up to see me, and the round-Ireland rally champeen, as he called himself, and I was given every football jersey there was in the League of Ireland to be hanging on my wall, it was like a lovely ould A-rab tent up there in my bedroom, and they never let a moment hurt me, and there was parish priests and nice ould rector women coming in and out, and didn't he have even an audience for me with the Pope himself all sorted, except that the ould sickness took a drag on me. And when I was laying there, more sicker than the sickest dog you ever seen, and them beside me, I never knew nothing but the pour of love off of them, and their hands on my head, and in particular my father's big hand on my head, like he could keep a lid on me, on my life, and not let me go too far that way. And the close close embrace he gev me, you would never think a human person could hold a person so soft, and he is a big ould giant of a person, isn't he?

Nicholas He is. And you were to see the Pope and all.

Girl I was to see the Pope, Nicholas Farquhar, and not only that, but didn't every single soul that lives hereabouts come up to my house, and my father lead every person that was wanting to visit me into the little room, and I was lying there panting for life right enough, that I might have been a foal just born in the danger of the snow. There was snow lying all about the world, and I was frosting into it, like a stone in the upshot that you can't pick up, it's that fastened by frost to the earth. And all the neighbours, all the neighbours of that earth, and strangers too come into the district, came up, and it was like a holy thing, I heard my father say that to Mammy, like a holy bloody thing it was, and I don't know if we were ever to know anything better than that, though at the end of the sentence of that tale was my goodbye. And I heard them telling stories, in whispers mostly, all through the night, and every night following, and at the end of the last bit of the last story was my goodbye.

Nicholas (*when he is sure she has finished*) That's it.

SCENE THREE

Music. On the cyc, the ewes peaceful with their lambs.

Nicholas in his chair. It might be the next day. The latch on the back door is lifted and someone comes, which Nicholas does register, but he doesn't seem alarmed. His sister Tania comes in; she's in her late forties, plump. She crosses quietly to the other chair and sits in it. Nicholas doesn't dare look at her.

Tania What did you do, Nicholas?

33

Nicholas I didn't do nothing that I know of. How is that boy?

Tania I can't ever come in here without thinking Mammy must be somewhere about.

Nicholas She's in the ould hospital in Naas.

Tania Nicholas.

Nicholas We'll have her home in jigtime, wait and you'll see. Don't you worry, Tania. She'll want to be seeing her daffodils making a start. Didn't she put them in herself, with her own fair hands, fifty year ago.

Tania Nicholas, you can't just be saying that all the time, it won't make her alive again just to be saying she's alive.

Nicholas You'd miss her all right. You'd miss her about the place, like you say. I suppose it's true she often used a sharp tongue to you. She was like a *sciog* under your arse sometimes. I know that. She was always on at you for that poor weak *óinseacháin* you married. God knows. But she can't even speak now, Tania, so we must speak well of her, until she comes home, and gets back to herself.

Tania The room is looking a bit dusty, Nicholas.

Nicholas I had some trouble with the fire. Jackdaws. They'd build a nest in your ear. Who's to see it?

Tania I saw some beautiful lambs in the upper field.

Nicholas Beautiful lambs.

Tania And the white heather looks so lovely on the hillside.

Nicholas Doesn't it though. (*A few moments.*) How's that boy then?

Tania It's not good news, Nicholas.

Nicholas No. How could it be. And him after lambasting the stomach off of himself.

Tania Andrew Stafford is full of grief. We went over last night to watch with him. They had left poor Evans where he was, you know. The whole of Ballycumber was there. He had someone bring in a big tea urn and Mags was making big beef sandwiches. It was very thoughtful. And the young lad was in his childhood room, with all the flags and posters of Liverpool around him, and he kept opening his eyes and seeing his poor father, and he says to him, 'I'm sorry, Dada.' That's all he was saying.

Nicholas He said nothing about me then?

Tania Not a word. But Andrew showed me the scrap of paper and what was wrote on it.

Nicholas He showed you that? And he showed everyone that, that was there? The whole of Ballycumber, and no doubt Crossbridge and all points east and west. The evidence.

Tania He showed me in quietness in the kitchen, when I was helping him fetch in sandwiches.

Nicholas Good for him.

Tania Because you're my brother, and he needs to know what it meant.

Nicholas And what did it mean?

Tania I don't know, Nicholas – what did you say to him here?

Nicholas I don't know what I said to him that would make him take out his father's old army gun and put a bullet in his own stomach.

Tania Nicholas. Don't cry.

Nicholas Like a childeen.

Tania Oh, we were both childeens in this house, and there was plenty to cry over then

Nicholas It wasn't so bad. Some had it worse.

Tania There's some things I can't ever get out of my head. There's this memory I have of Daddy, well, I have a few of them, but, it was in the snow, February maybe, and I was about four, in my dress, and we were outside together, him in his big boots, me in my leather shoes that Mammy got me that time, how do we remember things like that, and where are those shoes, because I think she kept them. There had been a new fall of snow and we were walking together up the short boreen to the house field, and I wanted him to hold my hand, or lift me up, that was the idea I had, and he was printing the snow with his boots, you know, and I was falling behind, and I was not saying a word, but I was greatly desiring, greatly, for him to turn his head and see my difficulty, just to turn his head, and take his eyes off the cattle or the sheep or whatever was in the field above us, but he wouldn't, I don't think he even had a thought for me there, a little girl in a dress with her good leather shoes, that couldn't manage the snow. And me struggling to keep up with him, to keep up with him. My father.

Nicholas Sure, what sort of memory is that? Wasn't he a farmer? He had to have a thought for his beasts in the snow.

Tania He was a farmer, and he was a father. Derek now dotes on our daughter. He is a lovely father, and in no manner a weak man. He is a man that had vicissitudes as a young fella himself, and he has overcome all that. He lost his mam and dad within the space of a year when he was nine.

Nicholas I know all that.

Tania Well, then, you should respect him, and not be taking your tune always from Mammy about him.

Nicholas Arra, Tania. Things were never so bad as you make out. You have a sort of *ochón-ochonó* about all them things. The old man was all right.

Tania He used to set me to sing on the counter of the pub like some little Shirley Temple, I remember that. I suppose that is a good memory, except he was probably drunk when he did it. But what does a little one know about that? And when I was big that time and I got the letter from the regional college that I had a place, I went into the pub with the letter, knowing well he wouldn't let me go, not ever, not for one minute, and he was there with the bank manager, and like a piercing blast of light in the brain I knew what to do, and I showed the bank manager the letter before Daddy, and the bank manager, being a normal decent human being, congratulated Daddy, so what could he do then, only pretend to be happy, and let me go.

Nicholas *Ochón-ochóno.* You want to cop on to yourself, Tania. Daddy needed you here. Mammy wasn't right in them days. Do you not remember the real fucking memories? Do you not remember, you and me maybe seven and eight or whatever, out in the garden, and Mammy on the sill of the window upstairs, hah, shouting that she was going to jump if her husband didn't come home that instant, and how were we to have him come home, were we magicians or what? Barking mad she was in them days, Tania.

Tania And do you wonder why, Nicholas? Think about it. An absolutely beautiful girl like that, from the poorest of the poor farmers of Leitrim, working in the pub in Shillelagh, and this big long toothy man coming in there drinking in his youth, and *plamásing* her into his life, on a high lonely farm like this. You pass her photograph every day in the hall, a beautiful fresh-faced woman, that had years and years then of his drinking and talking and going on. Years and years, an eternity.

Nicholas He wasn't so bad. He wasn't so bad. They were different times. And didn't he die then, and wasn't she much happier, hah?

Tania I don't know. Was she? It was you and her cooped up here. I got away.

Nicholas You got away, but you came back, didn't you? Nothing would do you but to be building a house nearby, the happiness you had to do that, and now look at you. He wasn't so bad.

Tania is crying now. Nicholas clicks his tongue.

Tania I'm sorry, Nicholas.

Nicholas stands up. He looks very angry.

Nicholas Come here to me.

Tania What?

Nicholas I said, come here, Tania.

Tania I'm not a little girl for you to be yelling at.

But she gets up anyway and goes to him. He looks like he might strike her.

Nicholas You're right.

Tania What?

He holds out his two hands to her. Indicates she's to hold them. She does.

Nicholas He was a terrible old fucker.

38

Tania Well.

Nicholas Maybe he didn't mean to be. He was a proud man, and it used to kill me to see him staggering in the town. It killed him. If ever a man died of shame at his own doings, it was Makepeace Farquhar. (*A moment.*) What sort of name was that for his father to give him?

Nicholas puts his arms around his sister a moment. Then he pushes her back gently and looks at her.

Britannia. What sort of fucking name was that to give you? Britannia.

Tania laughs.

Tania Oh, God.

Nicholas I don't know what to do about this thing. I want to be there with the rest of the district to help Andrew, but he doesn't want me down there. If Mammy was here she'd know a way round it. She was very good on the nature of the human being generally.

Tania Mammy's gone, Nicholas.

Nicholas I know.

A few moments.

Tania Evans passed away early this morning.

Nicholas Oh, Jesus, oh, dear.

Tania Thirty-six hours it took.

Nicholas It would, it would. Stomach wound. I seen it in slaughterhouses. Some *amadán* wouldn't know what he was doing. Even cattle have cries of pain, you know, the whole waiting herd feels it. But I don't know about the sorrow of cattle. There is no greater sorrow than the sorrow of a parent that loses a child. There is just none greater. God help and protect them.

Tania What did you say to him? Why is your name on the little note?

Nicholas I don't know.

Tania There wasn't anything amiss between you?

Nicholas What?

Tania Do you remember in the ould shop there at the edge of Crossbridge? Mammy said you weren't ever to go in there alone, and if you did, you were never to go behind the counter with Mr Kearney, because he had a bad name, and his own wife used to have to lock up his three sons so he couldn't get at them?

Nicholas I do remember that. (*A moment.*) Oh my Jesus – (*Pushing her away.*) Is that what you're thinking? Is that what Andrew is thinking? That I'm a sort of soulless man that would – Tania. Terrible words. Terrible thinking. I want Mammy. Bring in Mammy to me. Arra, my head is hurting now. Let her make the ould Alka-Seltzer. Make it fizz in the cup. Mammy? Come in to me. Please, please.

Tania I don't think it. I am saying what Andrew asked me, Nicholas.

Nicholas A fella up here with no wife, so you're thinking – my own sister, who knows me. (*Angry suddenly.*) You're coming up here, like a dreepy dry hogget in the lambing . . . (*Steadying himself, gentle again.*) I don't want the trouble of a woman, I seen enough of it here. I relish the peace of these days, till lately. He was my young friend. He liked to come in here talking. I gave him tea. I told him tales about this and that, ould shite from long ago, little things that happened to me in my life, he would sit there listening and laughing, and he came in freely, I never asked him, by the good Jesus, Tania, he was my good friend.

Tania I believe you, I'm sorry for upsetting you so, I am.

Nicholas Go way from me. I'm finished here in Ballycumber. Worries like them, they stick to a man. (*A moment.*) And the biggest thing of all is, the poor lad is dead. We should all be grieving, together. He is dead, so you say. But maybe he is not dead. You were wrong about Mammy. Maybe if you went down now to Staffords it would be very different. The lights on in the kitchen, and Andrew smiling and telling you about the great miracle, and how everything was so dandy now, and Evans after saying what he meant by the note, whatever it was. That's it, Tania. You go down now. Go down you to Staffords. Ah yes. That will be the proper story.

Tania I will go down, Nicholas, but I don't think anything will be very different.

Nicholas Go down away – you'll see.

Tania What's that there on the hearth, Nicholas?

Nicholas What? Oh. Instrument of warfare. An item to defend the Congolese with.

Tania Is that the gun that Evans used?

Nicholas It is. It is his father's gun. Andrew brought it over.

Tania Let me take it down to him.

Nicholas No, no, don't touch it. It's covered in blood. All sticky. Don't mind. I'll wash it off with a rag. I'll keep it for him. I will. That's what I'll do. I'll keep it for him, like a good neighbour.

Tania All right. (*Just before going.*) Look, Nicholas, I know you loved Daddy, and there was good things about him. It really depends how you tell the tale. When I was little and he used to take me into the pub and put me up on the counter to sing and dance like Shirley Temple, he really meant no harm. He would get a great hush going in the room, and he would demand utmost attention from his gathered friends, and I would perform my party piece with perfect happiness, *Baidin Fheilimi, d'imigh go Ghabhla, Baidin Fheilimi,'s Fheilimi ann*, and I felt like one of them halos in the Catholic church was on my head, and the gold streaming out of me, and my father golden too, with his smile as wide as Wicklow, and his own great and rare happiness.

She goes out.

Nicholas throws himself back into the chair and groans.

SCENE FOUR

Music. On the cyc, the fox takes a lamb from its mother and rends it.

Nicholas is on his own in the room, and it is dark night. There's a knocking on the door, which surprises him. He goes out to see who it is.

Nicholas (*off*) Is that you, man dear?

Nicholas comes back into the room. He is followed in by Evans, who goes and sits in his chair by the fire.

Were you not hurt at all then, Evans? I mean, did you come away from your wound?

Evans Well, she comes into my mind now and then, but I am learning to allow it. I am surprised I was let through the gate. When I came up yesterday there was a man there who barred me coming in.

Nicholas What man was that?

Evans I came up to the gate as always through fields that looked to me like Ballycumber, and there was a man there, and he said, 'You can't come in here now,' and I said, 'Who are you, I always come in here.' 'Well,' he said, 'you can't now,' and I said 'But I want to go in and see Nicholas,' and he said, 'No, you are not permitted.' And I said, 'There you are, standing at a country gate like a guard, there isn't even a gate on its hinges now, and I don't even know you, and I know every living soul in Ballycumber.' And he laughed at me, the hat on his head like a teetering chimney, and he said, 'You know me well enough, go on now and do what I bid you, there's the good man, and so there'll be no trouble.' But I said, 'I'm wanting to see Nicholas,' and he says, 'Ah sure, man dear, never you mind.' So I said to him, 'Do you know anything about the girl with the greeny-blue eyes,' and he says, 'Oh, do you mean Casey, the girl called Casey, that lives up past the school?' and I said, 'I don't know, is that her name, maybe so, but, sure there isn't anyone living up as far as that, isn't Cullen the last name and then there's no one?' 'Well,' he said, 'anyway, you can't come in here.'

Nicholas By sangs.

Evans So feeling much disconsolate since I had been looking forward to chewing the rag with you, I went on up the track as far as the ruined school. But the curious thing was, when I got nearer to it, you know how the road winds there among the beech trees, I heard singing come down the lane to me, it was children singing, and I got to the schoolhouse, and there was half of the building for boys, and half for girls, and I expect it was girls singing, because it sounded like that, high and sweet, and you know, it would make you feel a bit sad.

Nicholas Aye.

Evans And I must tell you, Nicholas, the little gardens were very shipshape and the master was growing lilies there and fuchsia and what have you, it was very like somewhere I had seen years ago, but where I couldn't tell you, and that old track usually so muddy and marked by old Cullen's tractors and whatever, was quite tamped down and cleared like a gang of men had been mending it, like it was a scar. (*A brief getsure towards his stomach.*) And they had come to heal it, and it was lovely walking there, on the green road, with the bellflowers there on the ditch, and all the ould *sciog* bushes trimmed and their thorns tamed. And I went to the bellflowers and I pinched one of the flowers and pressed it between thumb and index finger till it popped, and immediately I felt like a young chap again, going about.

Nicholas I know.

Evans And there was the drone of the bluebottles now and then, and the little mad crowd of black flies that follow your sweat in summer, and I went up higher on the track, marvelling the whole while, and all the ould houses that were let fall into disrepair were made all new again, and there were people in them, just straightforward men I saw in the fields with their sleeves rolled up, and the ridges on the fields from *gearróg* to *gearróg*, and a woman came to the half-door of the first house, and she smiled at me, and asked if I was thirsty, and would I take a cup of buttermilk. And I said I would gladly, and she went back into the shadows and brought a ladle for me to drink from, and she asked me my name, and I said I was one of the Staffords from Crossbridge, and she said she knew my family well, and her husband was a cousin of the Staffords.

Nicholas Well.

Evans So since we were easy there in the garden, with the geraniums as red as blood on the sills, and the big heads of blue flowers of the hydrangeas, and in the byre I could just see the wet noses of the calves, and I heard a pony stamping in the stable, and she had a little herd of Rhode Island reds in the yard, and the cock the gayest of all, and a black sheepdog asleep in a suntrap, and there was a girleen in the shadow of the dairy, and I could see her wet arms working in the gloom, with the wet paddles, patting out the butter, and she was singing, and (since we were easy there) I said to the woman at the door, after I was drinking the milk, and sweet cold thick stuff it was, that slaked the thirst, 'Do you know the girl called Casey with the greeny-blue eyes?' and she said, 'Oh yes, they have a little leaning house just up the valley,' she said, 'they are landservants of the Fitzwilliams.' And maybe I caught a little jump in her voice from the fact that I was going up to see Catholics.

Nicholas Oh.

Evans So I take my path up that way, and I come to a small curving field, and I see the house she had mentioned, and I went down through a broken gate, and there was no one there to bar my way. And I saw the girl in the yard in a very old-fashioned looking dress, just a sort of cotton summer dress with a blue and white polka-dot overdress over it, and just at that moment I raised my head and saw the smoke of all the houses on Ballycumber, every chimney had smoke, and every turn and narrow of the fields was tended, and everything good to the eye, and when she saw me she straightened, and she seemed to know me, and when I went down to her across the packstones of her yard, she was very content to take my hand and greet me, with the warmth of one who knew me as a follower.

He leans to the hearth and picks up the gun. He starts to clean it off with his sleeve.

Nicholas That's the best tale I ever heard told in Ballycumber. I am so glad you had that tale in you to be telling, and that I have heard it.

Evans My tale is not told yet, Nicholas. It has an ending to it. And here is the ending.

He replaces the gun on the hearth carefully, exactly as he found it.

I was standing there with the girl, and her hand in my hand, and my heart going like the clappers, and all from love of her, and I was very happy to be standing there, with the stir of the ladle of the breeze in the yard, and sun as yellow as soup, when up behind me from the track comes a couple of men, big bursting men they were in their dark suits, and a great cry from the girl that was called Casey, and the two men plucked me from her, and pushed me down on the ground, and one of the men had a sort of spike of a thing, and he drove it into my shoulder, and the other man had a pincers of a thing, and he pushed it into my trousers, looking for my poor balls, you know, and he, it was clear in that moment he wanted to castrate me, and I bellowed out since I had a bellow in me, and some other lads came round the cottage, maybe the girl's brothers they were, but when they saw me, they stopped there, laughing, and they told the girl to go into the house, and the first two black-suited men started to drag me off, and not a hand lifted to help me, and before I knew it I was pulled down to a set of barns, right there at the house of the woman that gave me the milk, and she was in the yard, 'You great big oligawn,' she said, 'did you think I'd let ya do that?' and they pulled me into the darkest barn, the darkest barn of all the world, and one of them took a black glistening gun that he had in an oily sack, and he looked me deep dark in the eyes, straight and personal as you like, and pressed the muzzle against my stomach, and me squirming to get away from it, and he laughed at my fear, and the piss that went coursing down my legs, and without another thought for himself or for me, he fired.

Nicholas looking at him for a few moments. Evans gets up, nods his head, and goes to the door.

Nicholas I don't see the wound, Evans.

Evans You could put your hand into it, it's such a size. You could warm a frozen pup in it.

Nicholas I don't see the blood, Evans.

Evans You could paint your letterbox with it, you could dye your handkerchief red with it, you could fill a black pudding with it like the blood of a pig. It would wash nothing.

Nicholas comes over to him and holds out his two hands.

Nicholas If I said anything, if I done anything to upset you, I am heartily sorry, Evans.

Evans I don't know what you said, Nicholas.

Nicholas I don't know what I said either. I have racked these stupid brains to remember what it was I might have upset you with. I have combed over the words in my head, but it is all mushy peas up there. It is like a big mess of a dinner, a hash.

Evans My father is always very fond of hash, surely, since because of his army days.

Nicholas Aye. In the Congo. And I know I have hurt that gossoon, and I am mad sorry for that, but how can I fix it, I don't know.

Evans The thing that breaks can't be put to mend.

Nicholas That's it. A stupid, blunted, wretched instrument is this man.

Evans So long, Nicholas.

He grips Nicholas's hands a moment.

Nicholas So long.

Evans (*going out*) Oh, Nicholas.

Nicholas Yes?

Evans Mind those jackdaws building in your house.

Nicholas Aye, I will, Evans, I will. Thank you.

Evans goes. Nicholas kneels at the fireplace. The gun is there.

Aye, I will, I will that. I will that. Forgive me, Mammy, for not being able to keep you alive. Forgive me for not being able to be happy now you are dead. I miss the cups of tea and the slices of cheese pulled off the wrappers and the talk. 'Will I move them heifers up to the upper garden?' 'Aye, do.' 'Will I put the road fields to tillage again, and grow barley, Mammy, or will I put them to setaside and get the EU money on them?' 'Well, well, you will do as you think best.' For I am a better farmer than my father. That is my legend. There was Nicholas Farquhar, a better farmer than his father. A drinking man who shamed his daughter, and shamed his wife, but never his son. No. Forgive me, Mammy, for the boil or rupture that was in your leg, and that crept up to your lung, and that hovered there and made you ill, and that weakened your heart, and that gave you the stroke then, and that took the whole left side from you, and you in the bed in Naas, and me saying, 'Will I move them heifers up to the upper garden?' and you talking double dutch back to me, and the love that is in me for you, very black then, black nights here alone, and not sorry truly, not sorrowing for you the way I should have been, but just sorrowing for myself like a small foolish man. I am a better farmer than

48

my father but I am not a better man. A son should be going marrying and bringing a young lady into the house to be rowing with the old woman. And then when the old woman dies, the son should know it, and not be believing otherwise, and hold his wife in the dark of the night, and feel her heat, and her life, and her honesty, and her duplicity, and her kindness, and her cruelty, and her love. And it should be all pristine and proper like that, so that when my young friend comes to me, with his heart heavy, and well I knew, I would know what to say to him, and not be offering only the tales of Ballycumber, but to have said something fresh and true to him, the best that I knew, so that his heart would have been solaced, and he would have gone from this house then to be asking for the girl with the greeny-blue eyes.

He puts the gun in against his stomach. He cocks the gun. The scrabble of a jackdaw in the chimney.

On the cyc, a new spring light grows. The yellow fire of the daffodils.

Evans appears indistinctly dressed as Elvis and silently and in slow motion dances in the darkest corner upstage.

The finches and robins start to sing.

Their music increases.

The girl comes out from under the table. She goes to Nicholas. He doesn't look at her.

She holds out a hand suddenly enough. She lays it on the top of his head. She leaves it there a few moments.

She goes off upstage (away up Ballycumber).

Nicholas with stiffness and a groan gets up. He trails over to the table. Lifting the gun closer to his face because of his eyesight, he uncocks it and puts on the safety catch carefully. He opens the drawer. For a moment he spots Tania's childhood shoes, takes them out, puts them back. Then he half fecks, half tips the gun in, and closes the drawer slowly with a finger.

Nicholas I'll keep that safe for you, I'll keep that safe for you.

Girl (*off*) Would you come on.

Evans goes off after her.

Music. Nicholas turns his face slowly towards the window (looking towards us). Light on his face more brightly. Just his private face. Slowly darkness. The daffodils burning deeper and brighter.